mel bay presents

Essential Jazz Lines

TENOR SAXOPHONE

in the style of **charlie parker**

by Corey Christiansen

This book of original musical studies and analyses by
Corey Christiansen is designed to help you develop your
own personal improvising style.

CD CONTENTS

1	Tune-Up [:29]	9	Long ii-V Moving In Fourths [3:17]	17	Short ii-V-I Moving In Fourths [3:17]
2	Minor Chord Vamp [2:39]	10	Major Vamp [2:12]	18	Long ii-V-I Vamp [2:34]
3	Minor Moving In Fourths [3:21]	11	Major Moving In Fourths [3:11]	19	Long ii-V-I Moving In Fourths [3:20]
4	Dominant Seventh Vamp [2:48]	12	Minor ii-V Vamp [2:14]	20	Minor ii-V-i Vamp [2:13]
5	Dominant Seventh Moving In Fourths [3:16]	13	Minor ii-V Moving In Fourths [3:13]	21	Minor ii-V-i Moving In Fourths [3:17]
6	Short ii-V Vamp [2:14]	14	Turnaround Vamp [2:05]	22	Byrd Blues Etude [1:50]
7	Short ii-V Moving In Fourths [3:18]	15	Turnaround Moving In Fourths [3:48]	23	Pent Up House [2:46]
8	Long ii-V Vamp [2:20]	16	Short ii-V-I Vamp [2:16]	24	Confirmation [4:15]

The companion play-along CD accommodates all of the versions available in the
Essential Jazz Lines In The Style of Charlie Parker.
Guitar Edition
Bass Clef Edition
E-Flat Edition
C Edition
B-Flat Edition

1 2 3 4 5 6 7 8 9 0

Visit us on the Web at www.melbay.com — E-mail us at email@melbay.com

Table of Contents

Charlie Parker

Charlie Parker was arguably one of the most influential jazz musicians to have ever lived. As the co-author of the bebop language (the musical language most jazz musicians are required to master), he and the other bebop musicians of the 1940's created a new way of approaching jazz improvisation. Much like the music of J.S. Bach, Charlie Parker's single note improvisations outlined the harmonies that were being used as a background.

This text presents numerous lines in the style of Charlie Parker. These lines have been grouped by the harmony they can be used against. Each idea or concept presented should be practiced with the accompanying play-along CD. After the line has been mastered in the key in which it is presented, it should be mastered in all twelve keys. For this purpose, each section has a chordal play-along that modulates around the circle of fourths. Ideas should be transposed and practiced with these modulating play-along recordings to ensure mastery in all twelve keys.

Some of the techniques used in the Charlie Parker style will also be discussed and examples shown. This will help musicians analyze each of the ideas presented; further insuring mastery of these ideas. It is hoped that many of these ideas will be assimilated into each student's musical vocabulary. More importantly, the student needs to understand how the style of bebop is played and the techniques presented in this book are assimilated to create original ideas.

Good luck and have fun learning this important style of jazz improvisation.

-Corey

Bebop Soloing

The bebop language, through the use of tension and release, outlines the harmony being played behind a soloist. Jazz is a type of music that glories in freedom. However, one needs to approach this type of music with certain rules that grant even more freedom. The freedom granted to players is the freedom of expression, an extension of freedom of speech.

The English alphabet has twenty-six letters. The letters A, E, I, O, U and sometimes Y are vowels, and all the other letters are consonants. Words cannot be built without vowels. It would be safe to say that vowels are the backbone of the English language. There are vowels, so to speak, in the musical language also.

While any chord is being played, all the notes in the musical alphabet (A, B, C, D, E, F, and G) and those with accidentals (sharps and flats) are fair game for soloing and/or creating melodies. However, some of these notes, if played for an extended period of time, might sound better than other notes (depending on the chord being played). These notes would be considered the "vowels," and all the other notes considered consonants. The "vowels" spoken of are chord tones. For example, if a C7 chord is being played, the notes C, E, G, and B♭ are the vowels. If a Dm7 chord is being played, the "vowels" are D, A, F, and C. All of the other notes act as "consonants" or "guides" to the "vowels." Non-chord tones provide a sound of instability or restlessness, thus creating a need for the stability provided by chord tones.

A portion of Charlie Parker's genius has to do with how he combined non-chord tones and chord tones to create timeless works of art. For this reason, a few of the techniques used by Charlie Parker are discussed in the following chapters.

Guide Tones

Guide tones are the notes in a chord which lead or give harmonic pull toward the next chord. A simple ii-V-I progression will demonstrate how guide tones work. In the ii-V progression, notice that the seventh degree in the Dm7 chord (C) leads to the third of the G7 chord (B) by a half step. The same can be seen in a V-I progression. The seventh of G7 (F) leads to the third of CMaj7 (E) by half step.

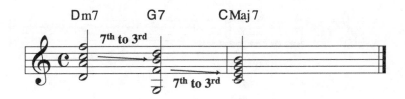

When soloing over ii-V-I progressions, Charlie Parker would often employ these guide tones. The example below shows how one might use this technique. By utilizing guide tones, a soloist is able to enhance the harmonic "pull" generated by the ii-V-I progression.

3

Bebop Scales

There are three basic bebop scales used by Charlie Parker. The Mixolydian (dominant seventh) bebop scale can be used primarily against dominant seventh chords. The Dorian bebop scale is used primarily against minor seventh chords. The major bebop scale is used primarily against major sixth and major seventh chords. Each of these scales is an eight-note scale rather than the typical seven-note scale. Because of their wide use in the improvisations of Charlie Parker, each of these bebop scales will be discussed separately.

The Mixolydian bebop scale differs from the Mixolydian mode in that it has an extra note between the root and the flatted seventh degree of the regular Mixolydian mode. This Mixolydian bebop scale is shown below.

Mixolydian Bebop
(played against dominant seventh chords)

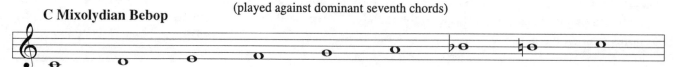

When a musician starts on a chord tone and plays this scale with eighth notes, each of the chord tones in a dominant seventh scale will be played on downbeats (strong beats). Because the bebop scales are eight-note scales, it takes exactly four counts to play each scale using eighth notes.

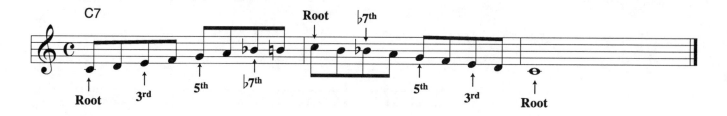

The following musical example shows how one might use this scale when soloing over a dominant seventh chord.

The Dorian bebop scale differs from the Dorian mode in that it has an extra note between the flatted third and fourth intervals of the regular Dorian mode. The Dorian bebop scale is shown below.

Dorian Bebop
(played against minor seventh chords)

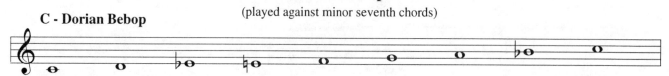

The Dorian bebop scale is an eight-note scale and will take exactly four beats to play if eighth notes are employed. However, not all of the chord tones of the respective minor seventh chord will be played on downbeats if one starts on a chord tone. Charlie Parker utilized this scale by starting on the fourth of the chord (a G note when playing against a Dm7) and leading to the third (F) chromatically. An example of how one would use this technique is shown below. It is also arguable that Charlie Parker may have been treating minor seventh chords as a dominant seventh chord a fourth away. This means he would have been playing G7 material against Dm7 chords.

The major bebop scale differs from the major scale in that it has an extra note between the fifth and sixth degrees of the regular major scale. The major bebop scale is shown below.

Major Bebop

(played against major seventh chords)

Like the other bebop scales, the major bebop scale is an eight-note scale and will take exactly four beats to play if eighth notes are used. If one starts on a chord tone and plays this scale utilizing eighth notes, each of the chord tones in the respective major sixth chord will be played on downbeats. An example of how one might use this scale to improvise is shown below.

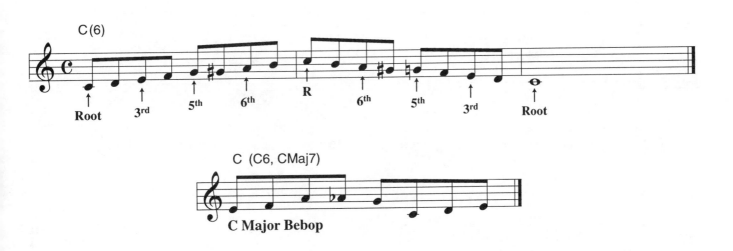

3 to ♭9

Three to flat nine is a technique that Charlie Parker used over dominant seventh chords. Most great jazz soloists are aware of this sound and have used it at one time or another. If the chord being played is a G7, the third is B and the flat nine is an A flat. There are a number of ways to get from the third to the flat nine. The first and most obvious way is by skip. Move from the third and ascend to the flat nine or move from the third and descend to the flat nine. Examples of this are shown below.

Another way to get from the third to the flat nine is by way of a diminished arpeggio. A diminished seventh arpeggio consists of nothing but minor third intervals. To build a diminished seventh arpeggio from a G7 chord, start with the third of the G7 (B), and then play a D (moving up or down). Next, ascend or descend to the minor seventh of the chord (F). From the F, ascend or descend to an A flat. The direction of the arpeggio doesn't have to start and continue in only one direction. In fact, it sounds interesting when the direction changes.

The third to flat nine sounds good when a dominant seventh chord resolves to a major chord a fourth away (G7-Cmajor). In the case of G7 to C, the flat nine (A♭) leads to a G note, which is the fifth of a C, major chord.

The lines found below show how one might use this technique in a V-I chord progression.

It is important to practice these techniques in all twelve keys. With practice, this material will flow effortlessly while improvising.

Playing the Upper-Structure of Chords
(Secondary Arpeggios)

Another technique used by Charlie Parker when improvising is arpeggiating the upper-structure of chords. The upper-structure of a chord is any note in the chord above the seventh. For example, a Cmaj7 chord consists of a root (C), major third (E), perfect fifth (G), and major seventh (B). These notes are derived from the C major scale. The upper-structure chord-tones (extensions) of the Cmaj7 chord are the ninth (D), eleventh (F), and the thirteenth (A). The way in which these notes relate to the major scale is shown below.

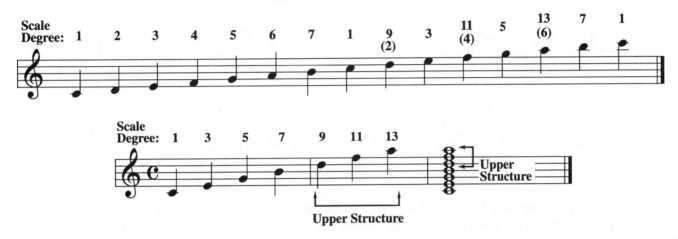

Charlie Parker would often start on the third of a chord and arpeggiate up to the ninth. An example of how this technique would be used against a D minor seventh chord is shown below.

Notice the notes from this example are the same notes contained in an Fmaj7 chord. Standing by itself, the upper-structure of any chord will create another chord. This is why the term secondary arpeggio is sometimes used to describe this technique.

Shown below are the secondary arpeggios for the basic chords in a major ii-V-I progression.

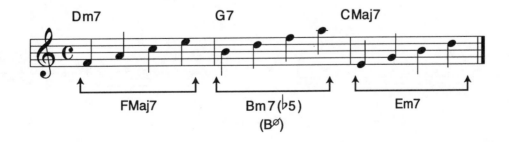

Targeting

Another technique Charlie Parker used that is covered in this book is called targeting. Targeting has to do with approaching chord tones by scale tone or chromatically. There are a number of ways to target a chord tone. The first is by ascending and descending chromatic approach. This technique is shown below. It is important to realize that while the examples shown below use the chord tones from a C major chord, this technique may be used over any type of chord (minor, dim, etc.). (Notice the notes are arranged so the chord tones are played on the downbeats.)

The next type of targeting is to use what many call an "enclosure." An enclosure uses either scale tones above and below or chromatic tones above and below to literally enclose a chord tone. For each of the sequences of notes discussed, the order of non-chord tones may be reversed.

The first type of enclosure makes use of a scale tone above and a chromatic tone below.

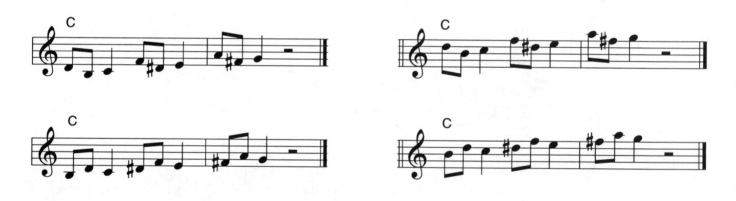

The next type of enclosure uses a scale tone below and a chromatic tone above.

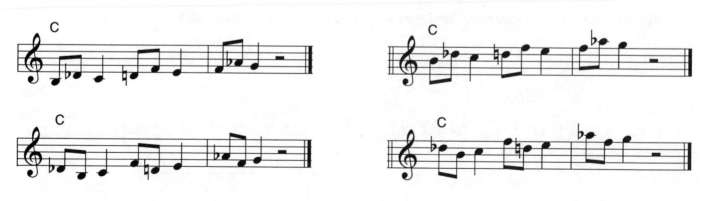

* If any examples in the book are written in the wrong register for your instrument, simply move the musical idea up or down an octave.

Three note enclosures combine scale tones above and below as well as chromatic tones above and below. A few examples of how this would apply to the root of a C major chord are shown below. Use this concept with all the other chord tones.

By combining scale tones and chromatic tones to enclose a chord tone, almost limitless possibilities of improvised lines may be constructed. Experiment with these combinations to create original lines.

The following line demonstrates how one might use the technique of targeting.

By learning these techniques, any musician will find it easier to analyze, memorize, and execute the lines provided in this book as well as lines from any transcribed solo. These techniques and lines will help musicians assimilate the bebop language into their own playing. The student should select a few lines for each harmonic situation and master them by playing them in all twelve keys with the accompanying play-along CD. By "plugging" the following Charlie Parker style lines into a solo and mastering the techniques presented in this book, each student will eventually master the jazz language and develop their own style and sound.

Minor Chord Material

For this section, the student must select a line to master, practice it in the given key with the accompanying play along CD and then use the CD track that modulates in fourths to master the line in all twelve keys. By combining minor chord lines with dominant seventh chord material, musicians will be able to mix and match numerous combinations of these lines to play over the ii-V-I progression. Because the major and minor ii-V-I are the most common chord progressions in jazz, it is crucial that students of jazz improvisation are fluent in soloing over this progression in all twelve keys. Because horn players frequently play in flatted keys, the material presented in this section of the book is in the key of B♭.

Minor Chord Vamp

Dm7

Minor Moving In Fourths

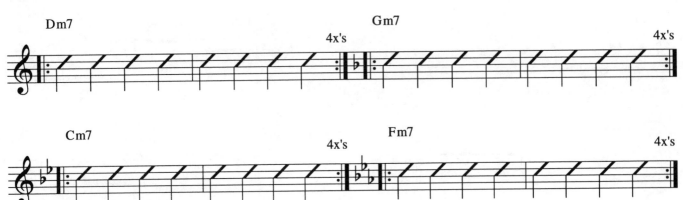

Dm7   Gm7   4x's   4x's

Cm7   4x's   Fm7   4x's

B♭m7   4x's   E♭m7   4x's

A♭m7   4x's   C#m7   4x's

F#m7   4x's   Bm7   4x's

Em7   4x's   Am7   4x's

Dominant Seventh Chord (V) Material

13

Dominant Seventh Vamp
 CD #4

Dominant Seventh Moving In Fourths
 CD #5

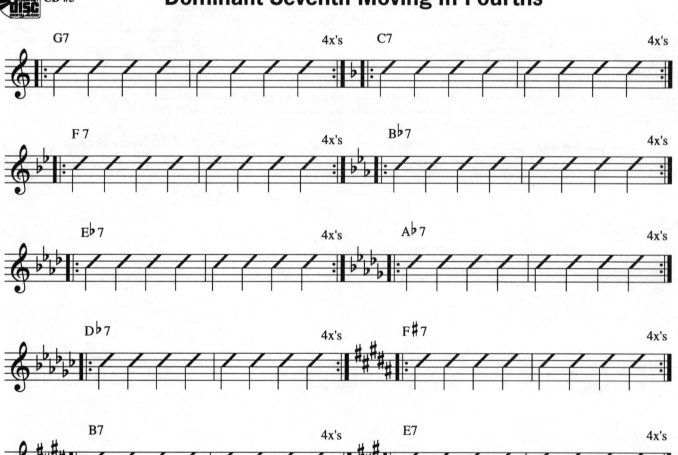

One Measure ii-V (Short ii-V) Material

Short ii-V Vamp

Short ii-V Moving In Fourths

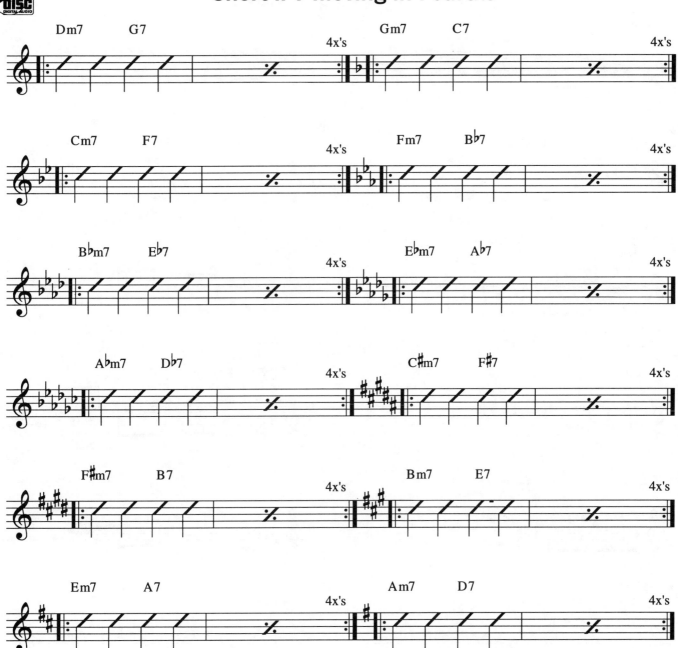

Two Measure ii-V (Long ii-V) Material

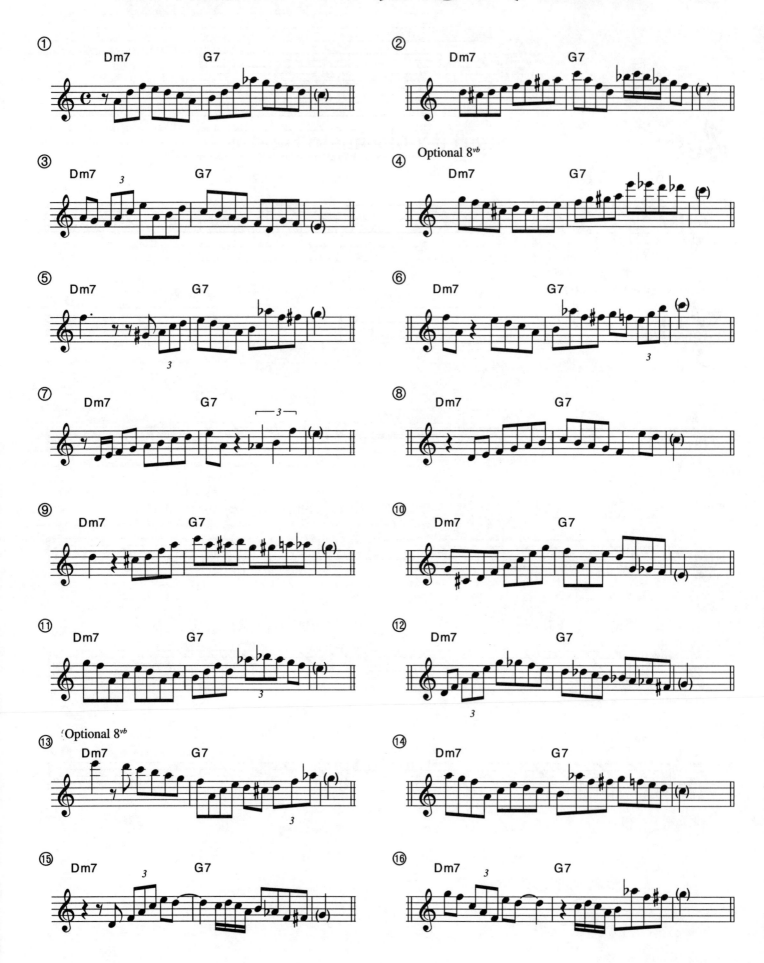

 CD #8

Long ii-V Vamp

 CD #9

Long ii-V Moving In Fourths

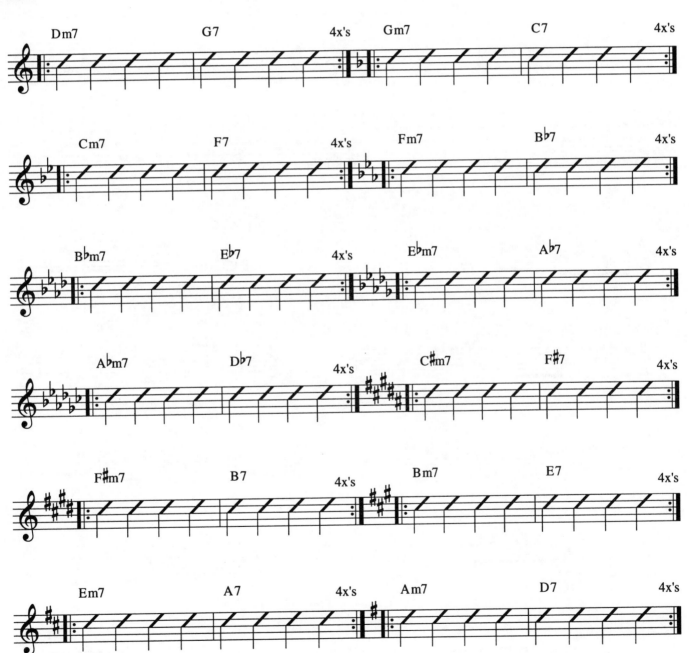

Major Chord (I) Material

Major Vamp

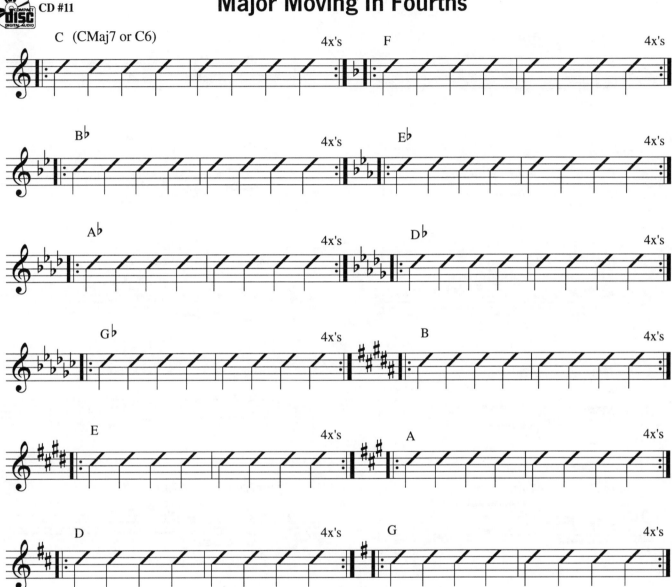

Major Moving In Fourths

Minor ii-V Material

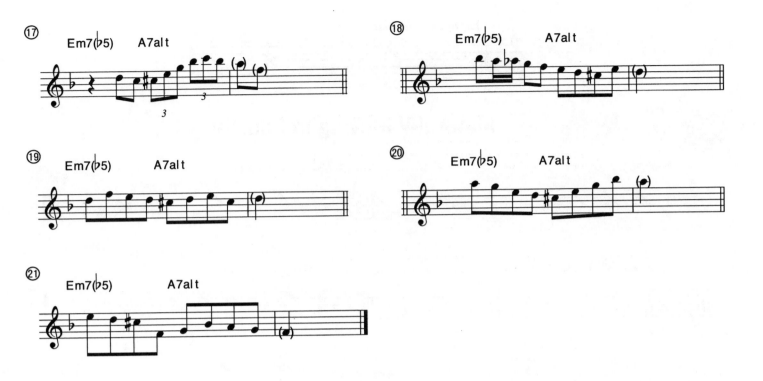

* For long (two-measure) minor ii-V progressions, either combine two short minor ii-V lines or expand the material for each chord in the progression.

TIP: Charlie Parker often played the harmonic minor scale for minor ii-V progressions a whole-step lower than the ii chord. (C harmonic minor against Dm7♭5 and G7alt.)

Minor ii-V Vamp

Minor ii-V Moving In Fourths

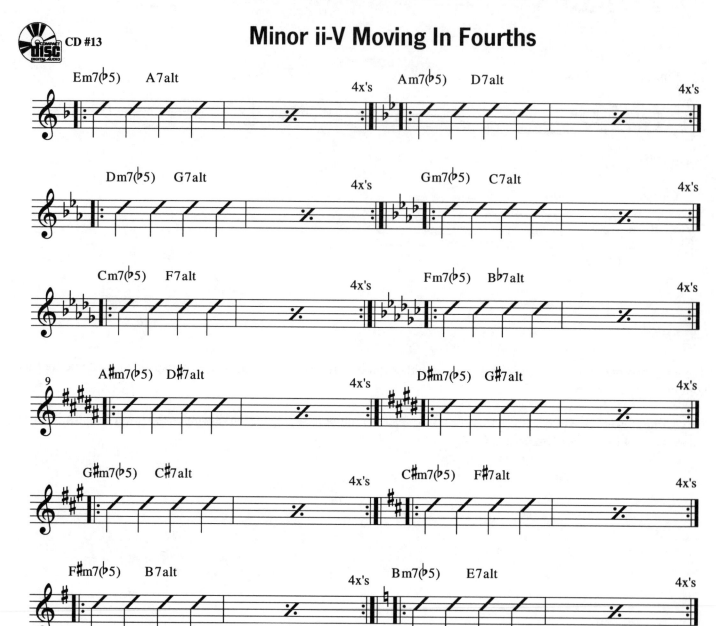

Turnarounds

A common turnaround in jazz consists of a minor ii-V leading to a major ii-V. The major ii-V resolves to the tonic major chord. The turnaround occurs two measures before the progression resolves to the tonic chord. Because many tunes start with the tonic, the turnaround is commonly found in the last two measures of a tune. The chords Em7♭5, A7alt, Dm7, and G7 make up a turnaround in the key of C. This progression is shown below. By combining lines that work over a minor ii-V progression with major ii-V lines, one can easily construct lines that work well over a turnaround. The examples shown below illustrate how to combine minor and major ii-V lines to improvise over a turnaround.

Practice combining minor and major ii-V lines to solo over the following turnarounds. The following turnarounds are recorded on the accompanying CD.

CD #14

Turnaround Vamp

CD #15

Turnaround Moving In Fourths

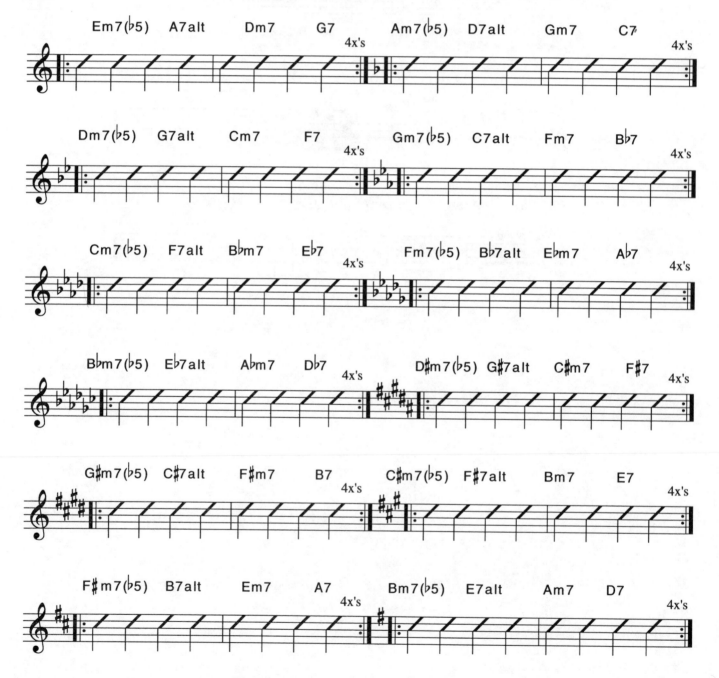

Use the following play along recordings to practice combining material for major and minor ii-V-I progressions. Use the material provided in the minor chord section, dominant seventh chord section, short ii-V section, long ii-V section and major chord section. The possibilities for creating new combinations are limitless.

Short ii-V-I Vamp

CD #16

Short ii-V-I

CD #17

27

 CD #18

Long ii-V-I Vamp

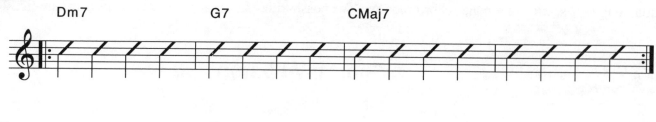

 CD #19

Long ii-V-I

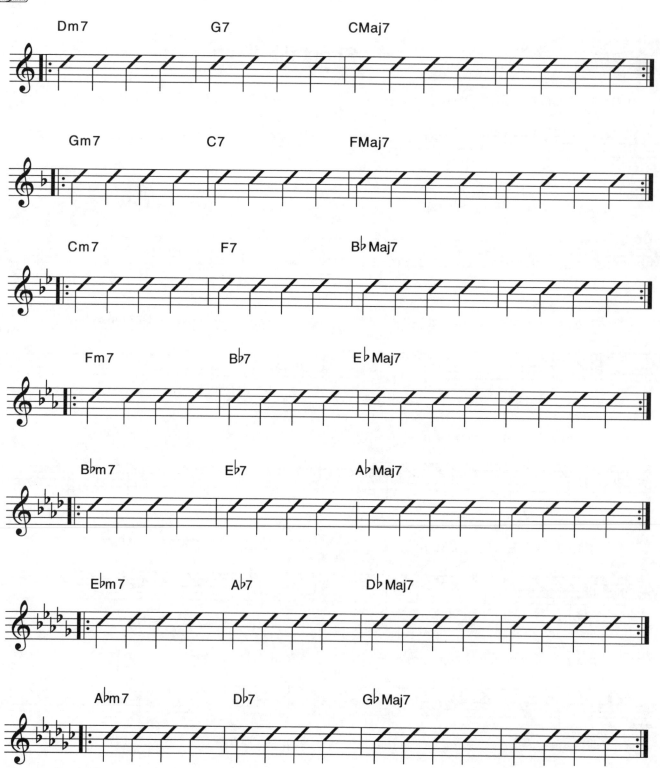

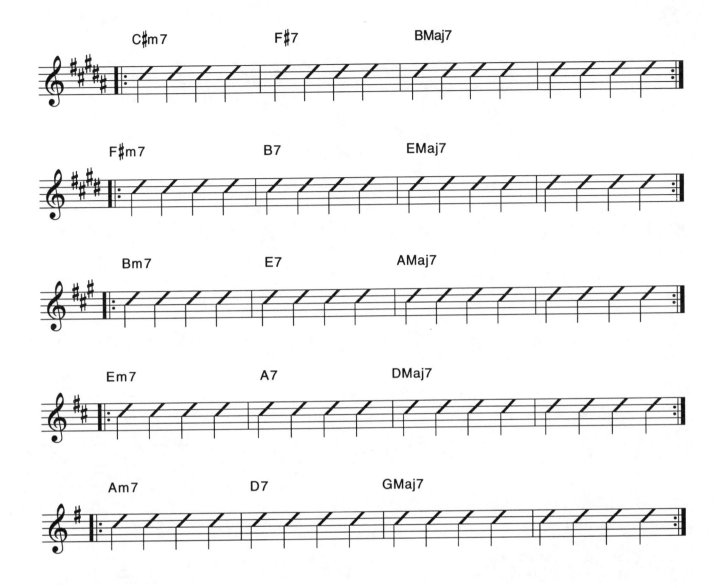

Minor ii-V-I Vamp

Minor ii-V-I

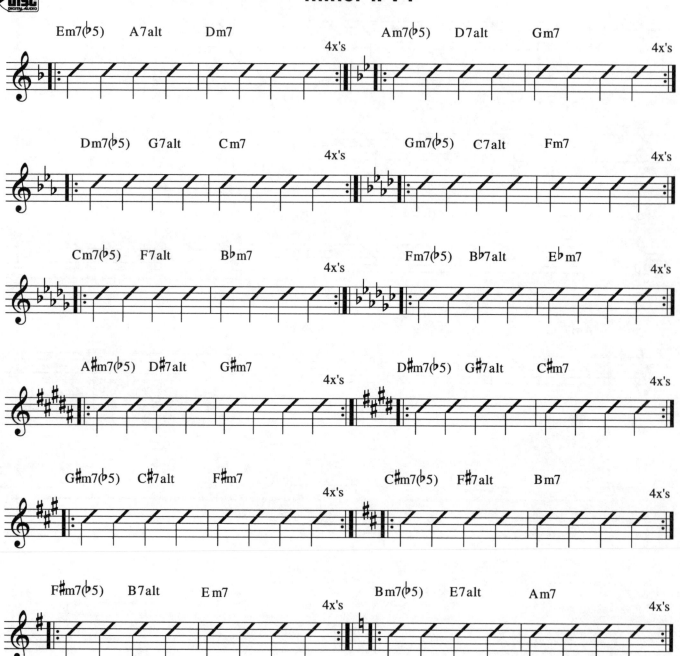

The following etude demonstrates how the lines and variations of the lines from the book can be used to create an improvised solo.

The following progressions are similar to the jazz standards "Pent Up House" and "Confirmation." Each of these progressions will make use of ii-V-I progressions. The progression similar to "Confirmation" also uses minor ii-V progressions. Using material from this book, practice improvising to these chord progressions.

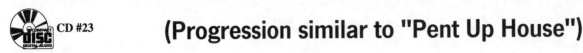

(Progression similar to "Pent Up House")

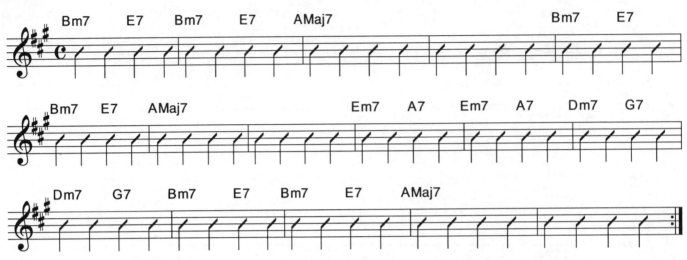

(Progression similar to "Confirmation")

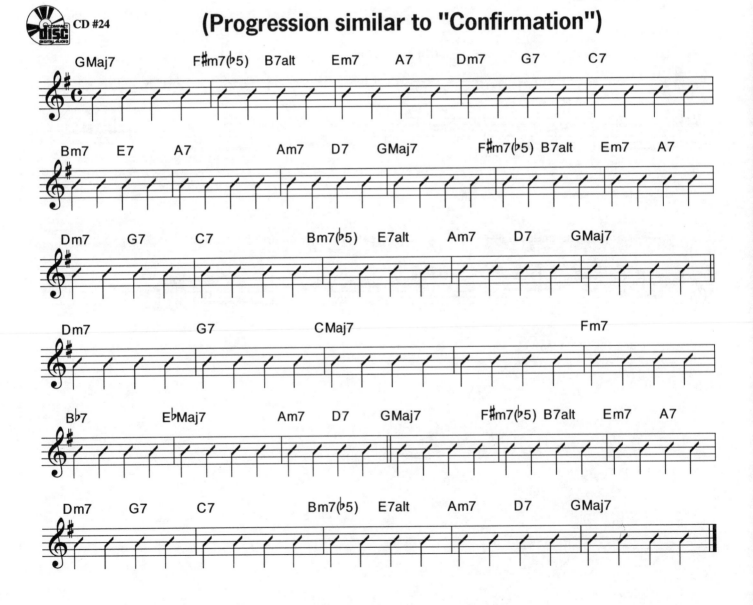